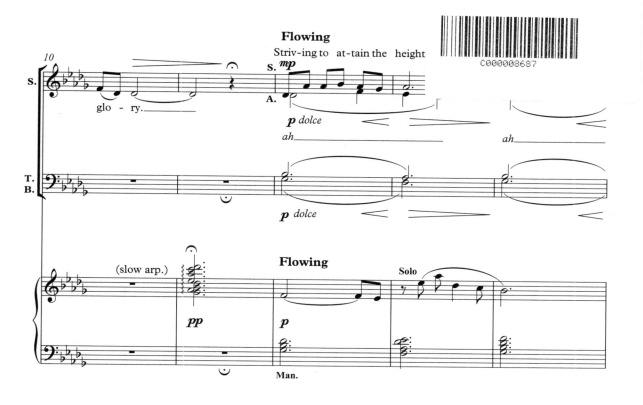

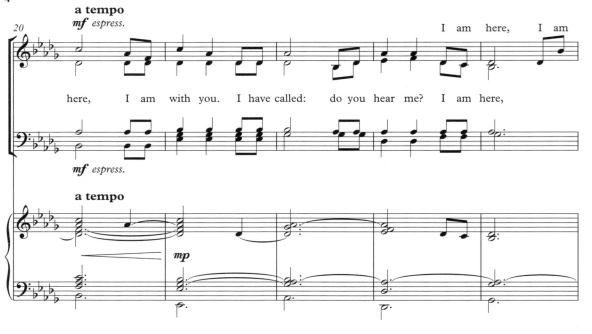

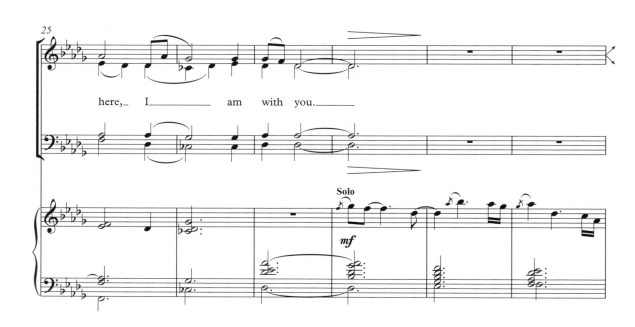

ANTHEMS

General Editor David Willcocks

SATB and organ

The Call of Wisdom

Will Todd

MUSIC DEPARTMENT

OXFORD
UNIVERSITY PRESS

*Commissioned by the Chapter of St Paul's Cathedral for the Diamond Jubilee of HM The Queen,
with generous sponsorship by The Worshipful Company of Horners*

The Call of Wisdom

Michael Hampel (based on Proverbs 8)

WILL TODD

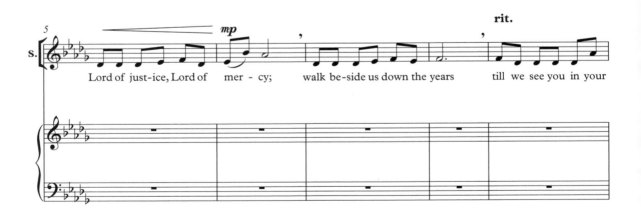

The Call of Wisdom (upper voices version) was performed at St Paul's Cathedral on 5 June 2012 in the presence of HM The Queen and HRH The Duke of Edinburgh.

This anthem is also available in an arrangement for upper voices and organ (ISBN 978-0-19-338972-4).

OXFORD UNIVERSITY PRESS, MUSIC DEPARTMENT, GREAT CLARENDON STREET, OXFORD OX2 6DP

Sil - ver, gold,

Sil - ver is of pass-ing worth, gold is not of con-stant va - lue,

Sil - ver, gold,

Sil - ver is of pass-ing worth, gold is not of con-stant va - lue,

Man.

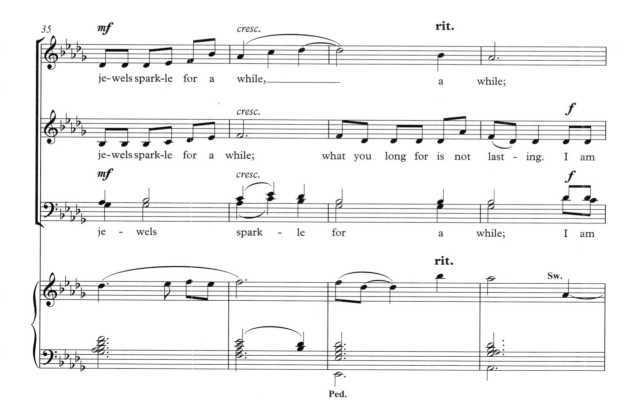

je-wels spark-le for a while, a while;

je-wels spark-le for a while; what you long for is not last - ing. I am

je - wels spark - le for a while; I am

Sw.

Ped.

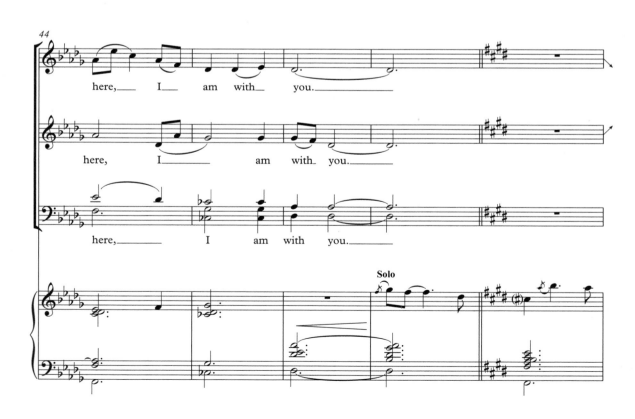

Ru - lers go-vern un - der me with my in-sight and my wis - dom.

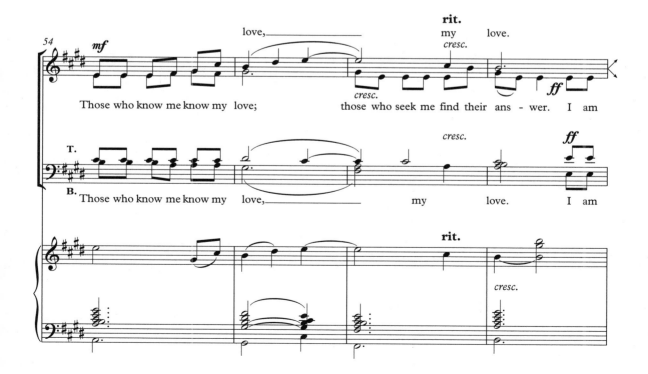

love, my love.

Those who know me know my love; those who seek me find their ans - wer. I am

Those who know me know my love, my love. I am

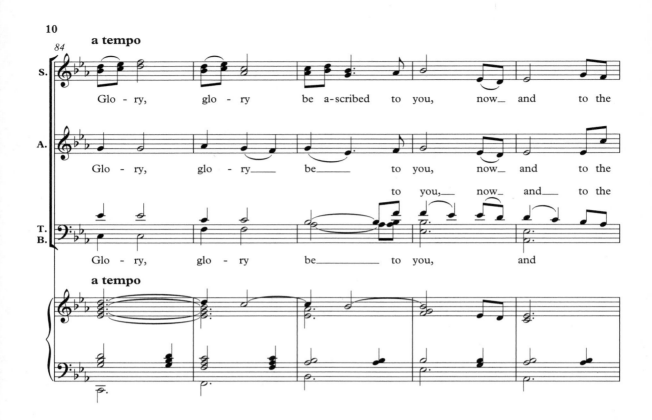

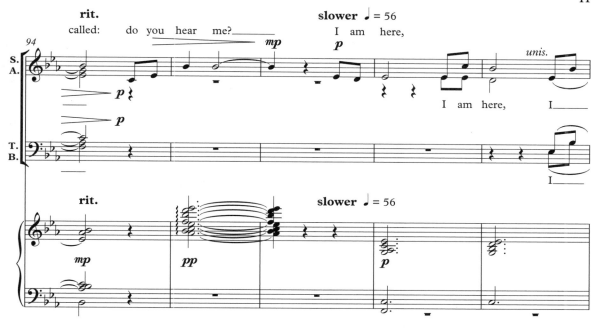

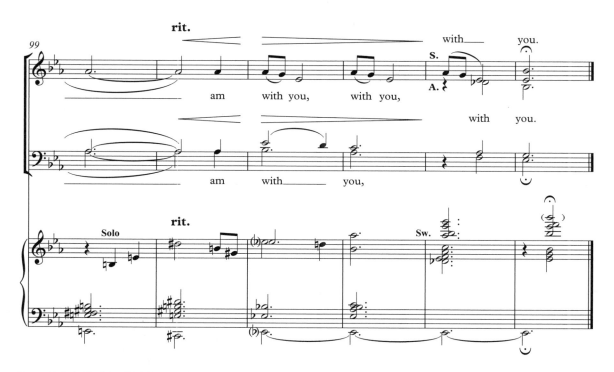

Processed in England by Enigma Music Production Services, Amersham, Bucks.
Printed in England by Halstan & Co. Ltd, Amersham, Bucks.

X544 **The Call of Wisdom** TODD

OXFORD

UNIVERSITY PRESS

www.oup.com

ISBN 978-0-19-339031-7

9 780193 390317